On Understanding Russia

As an outstanding educator and economist, Dr. F. Cyril James is particularly well qualified to observe modern Russia, and to comment upon it for Western readers. While he disclaims any right to speak with authority on the basis of his recent tour, the reader will quickly realize that he was actually given exceptional opportunities to see Soviet life, economy, and education—visiting some places that few foreigners have seen—and that, as a trained observer, he was able to draw fully from his experiences.

As Dr. James points out, "it is imperative that we should learn all that we can about the U.S.S.R. in order to understand its people—their habits, their ambitions, and their thoughts." He describes most vividly how the system of research institutions and university education provides incentive and then a very fully occupied life for those who are gathered into it. The comparisons of university budgets, salaries, and student expenses with those of North America are revealing. Dr. James tells also of the interesting developments from Mr. Khrushchev's proposal that students should work in factories or on farms before going on to university.

F. CYRIL JAMES was born in England, and received his B.Com. degree from the University of London. He took his A.M. and Ph.D. degrees at the University of Pennsylvania, where he taught from 1924 to 1939, becoming Professor of Finance and Economic History in 1938. In 1939, Dr. James was appointed Director of the School of Commerce at McGill University, and in 1940 he became Principal and Vice-Chancellor of McGill.

Dr. James has been awarded many honorary degrees by universities in Canada and abroad; he is a Fellow of the Royal Society of Canada; he has served with distinction on many boards and committees; and he is the author of well-known works on economic subjects.

T0335326

On Understanding Russia

F. CYRIL JAMES

Copyright, Canada, 1959
by University of Toronto Press
Reprinted 2017
ISBN 978-1-4875-9201-1 (paper)

Preface

THIS IS NOT A NEW REPORT ON RUSSIA. A MONTH IN THE
U.S.S.R. does not give a man the right to speak with
authority and, in my own case, the experience has taught
me how much I still have to learn, how many details of
Soviet life and of the Soviet economy I know little or nothing
about.

The seven articles in the following pages are no more than
a series of personal impressions and opinions. They are
reprinted in substantially the form in which they first appeared in the *Montreal Daily Star*, but I have taken advantage of the opportunity to correct minor errors and to add
some statistical information from which the reader can draw
his own conclusions.

My colleagues on the journey were President and Mrs.
Harlan Hatcher, Professor William Dewey and Mr. Lyle
Nelson (all of the University of Michigan), President and
Mrs. Norman Auburn of the University of Akron and Mr.
William Pine of the Ford Motor Company. To each of them
I owe much because any reader who follows our course on
the map will realize that we travelled far, visiting some places
that few foreigners have been to and encountering the usual
mixture of discomforts and delights. In such circumstances

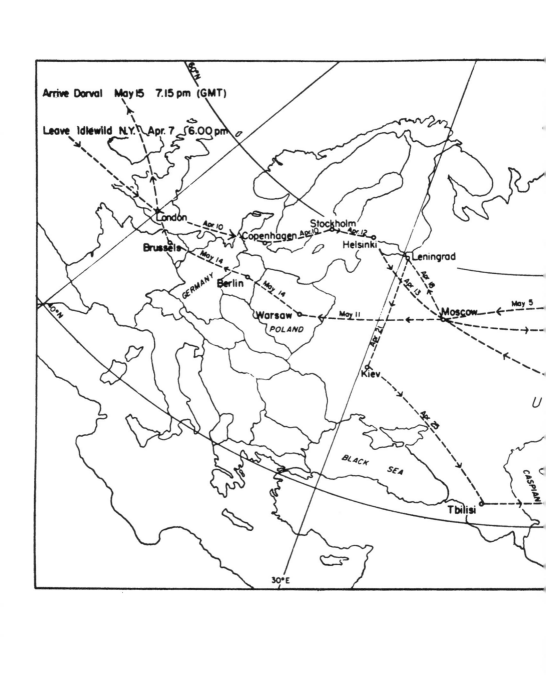

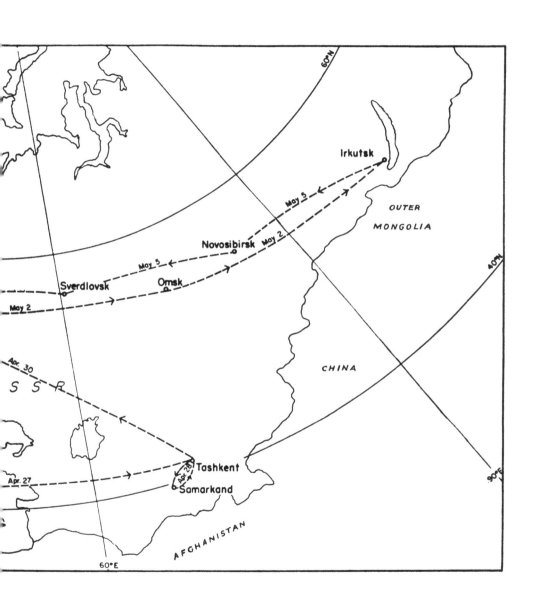

one learns to know and appreciate one's travelling companions and, although I am indebted to each, I should like to express particular appreciation of Harlan Hatcher, our leader, William Dewey, our indefatigable translator whose fluency in Russian won high compliments, and Lyle Nelson, our organizer and trouble-shooter on whose shoulders many of our problems came to rest.

My debt to the Ford Foundation which financed our journey, to the Government of the U.S.S.R. which received us with cordiality, and to our academic hosts at each of the institutions we visited, is beyond computation. What merit there is in these articles is due in no small measure to all of those whom I have mentioned. The errors, opinions and appraisals are my own.

F. Cyril James

August 1959

Contents

On Understanding Russia

1. Introduction

IT IS IMPOSSIBLE TO UNDERSTAND MODERN RUSSIA EXCEPT IN terms of the long centuries of her history, which runs backward for more than a thousand years to the founding of Kiev, Vladimir and Moscow—in each of which cities the present government is jealously preserving the historic monuments of the past. The October Revolution of 1917 changed many things, and the rate of change has become increasingly dramatic during the last ten years, but economic policy, social life and a good deal of foreign policy in our own generation are strongly influenced by historical forces that were worrying the governments of western Europe a century ago, at the time of the Crimean War: the Russian penetration of Persia and the spread of Russian imperialism in Asia to the very borders of Afghanistan and China. To make a true appraisal of the U.S.S.R. today one must read such books as Sir Donald Mackenzie Wallace's *Russia*, first published in 1877 and continuously revised until the last edition in 1912, and Sir Henry Norman's vivid impressions in *All the Russias* which was first published in 1902. The autocracy of the Czars appeared as permanent as time itself when these books were written, but many of their pages are as contemporary as today's newspaper.

3

We tend to forget the past, I think, because we unconsciously accept the Soviet propaganda that emphasizes Communism and, quite naturally, tries to suggest that every significant development in Soviet life or Soviet policy has come to birth since the Revolution. Such unconscious acceptance beclouds our long-range judgments. We must appraise Communism in its modern Russian context, not as an ideology in theoretical textbooks.

Communism is a new force in the world, and Russia believes in Communism. There is no doubt about that. Mr. Anastasias Mikoyan, when he received us in the Kremlin shortly before our departure from Moscow, opened the discussion by pointing out that Russia differed from western countries in believing that Karl Marx had formulated the philosophy which would, in the long run, appeal to the minds of all men throughout the world. This ultimate victory of Communism, he emphasized, was not a matter of military conquest but of intellectual conviction. Many generations might pass before all men became convinced, but ultimate conversion, in his opinion, and that of most Russians, is inevitable. Mr. Mikoyan was merely stating briefly, and cogently, the idea that seems to lie at the back of the minds of all the people we met in the U.S.S.R. During the May Day parade, hundreds of thousands of the citizens of Moscow marched through the Red Square of the Kremlin carrying banners which, without exception, proclaimed the virtues of Communism and the devotion of the people to that ideal. Throughout the city of Moscow, and indeed throughout all the other cities of the U.S.S.R. that we visited during the days immediately before the May Day celebrations, large pictures of Karl Marx (looking extraordinarily like a benign Santa Claus) decorated the walls. There seemed to be even more pictures of Karl Marx than there were of Lenin, the other Patron Saint of Communism who, with Trotsky, was the effective founder of modern Russia.

It should also be pointed out that 80 per cent of all the people now living in the U.S.S.R. attended school since the October Revolution of 1917, so that their education has a Communist flavour and their personal experience has been limited to the environment of the present Soviet society. Each student who attends any institution of higher education, no matter whether he is studying physics, philosophy or physical education, is required during the five-year curriculum that leads to his diploma to take a series of "required courses" that are taught by professors specifically chosen and appointed by the Ministry of Higher Education. During the first two years he takes a sequence of courses labelled "The History of the Party," which describe the origins of Communism, the Russian Revolution and the subsequent reorganization of the country. During his third year he takes a course in political economy which outlines the structure and operation of the present Soviet economy, and this is followed in his fourth year by a course on dialectical materialism. The final course, in the fifth year, covers the other half of Karl Marx's philosophy, historical materialism.

All Russians, and particularly educated Russians, have therefore learned, and accepted as a part of the climate of opinion in which they live, the basic pattern of Communist philosophy. If they were open and avowed anti-Communists they would have little chance of a successful career or a comfortable life. No foreign newspapers, magazines or books are allowed to enter the U.S.S.R. excepting those destined for the libraries of research institutions. Very few foreign moving pictures are shown, and few people have access to radio broadcasts emanating from other countries. For most of the inhabitants of the U.S.S.R. Communism is, therefore, the only philosophy that they know and the planned economy in which they live is the only pattern of life with which they are familiar. In this sense the Iron Curtain is more effective than any other international boundary that I have ever crossed.

Any commentary by a western visitor who has been in Russia must begin with recognition of this fact: that Russians believe Communism to be the best and most perfect philosophy, and the realization that no Russian outside the small highly educated minority has any personal knowledge of what goes on, of what men live for and are willing to die for, outside the Iron Curtain.

We must recognize this fact and live with it. The western world, even if it wished to do so, could not conquer the U.S.S.R. in order to eradicate Communism—any more than Christendom at the time of the Crusades was able by military force to interrupt the development of Islam. Force, and the threat of force, do not make a man change his philosophy or his religion. They tend to make him more stubbornly convinced.

In my personal opinion, Communism is neither perfect nor is it likely to be the dominant philosophy of the future. Christ gave two commandments that enshrine the essence of Christianity. "Thou shalt love the Lord thy God with all thy heart, with all thy soul, and with all thy mind . . . and thy neighbour as thyself." Communism, at its ideal best, which all intelligent Russians admit to be quite different from what exists in the U.S.S.R. today, concentrates its attention on the second of these commandments, to the exclusion of the first, but it is as true today as it was two thousand years ago that "man shall not live by bread alone." Much of the force of the arguments that Karl Marx put forth a century ago is to be found in the suffering and distress of millions of men and women, in the industrial conditions of the nineteenth century, rather than in the logic of his presentation.

The U.S.S.R. believes in the ultimate coming of Communism in the same way that true Christians look towards the millenium—the kingdom of Christ on earth—but no Russian suggests that the U.S.S.R. has already attained to a perfect Communist society, or is likely to in the near future. What exists in the U.S.S.R. today is an efficient, and carefully planned, state socialism—as far from true Communism as western society is from that perfect state of Christianity to which the Patristic Fathers looked forward. Russia is still Russia, and the government has to use the kind of inducements that western capitalism uses. Economic initiative is encouraged by high salaries and generous bonuses. On the collective farms, energetic and efficient workers are encouraged by the payment of salaries much higher than those paid for the less exacting tasks. In tens of thousands of factories, in all parts of the country, management is encouraged to reduce costs of production in order that there shall be as large a margin as possible between those costs and the selling price that is fixed by the central planning organization. This margin, or profit, is available for the payment of bonuses not only to management but also to key workers, and a part of it is invariably used for the benefit of all the workers in the factory. In terms of daily life, therefore, these operations are not very different from comparable activities in the western world.

It must also be remembered that the active and enthusiastic members of the Communist party comprise a small percentage of the total population of Russia. The others simply accept the dominant philosophy, and I remember an able young teacher in one of the required courses who complained to me that his students were not as interested in his subject as they were in their own specialties of technology and the physical sciences. It sounded very much like the complaints of Canadian professors who are charged with the responsibility for teaching economics to engineering students or English literature to those whose enthusiasm is for chemistry or physics.

We in the West cannot ignore Communism, any more than Christendom could ignore Islam a thousand years ago. But the practical problems of life—then and now—are just as important as the dominant philosophy which men often accept most readily when they understand it least. I like to remember that, during a later war of religious fervour that is part of our own family history, when the great Armada of Spain was sailing up the Channel to destroy Protestant England, the "Bloody Question" on the answer to which a man's life might depend was not any theological inquisition regarding Protestantism or Roman Catholicism. It was: *"Do you fight for England or do you fight for Spain?"*

To my mind the basic question is just as blunt today. Will Russia work, and fight, to preserve and develop the great heritage of western civilization—which is hers as well as ours —or will she endeavour to destroy it? I do not know the answer—but I do know that the answer will determine the pattern of the lives of our children's children. It is important, therefore, that we should break through the cloudy arguments about Communism and try to understand the minds, the habits, and the ultimate ambitions, of the Russians. This is my purpose in these articles, and I shall avoid as far as possible any thrashing of the old straw of Communism versus capitalism.

When we look at the U.S.S.R. from this angle, it is at once apparent that we have a lot to learn before we can arrive at any rational appraisal. The U.S.S.R. is a federation of fifteen republics—many of them with a language and literature vastly different from those of Russia—which occupies a territory that is three times as large as Canada.

Russian society, moreover, is a thousand years older than Communism and some of the things that irritate foreign visitors—such as the internal passport, the limitations on personal freedom and the restrictions on travel—are inherited by the Soviet government from the older administrative organization of the Czars.

As early as the ninth century, trade was moving profitably along the Varangian Route from Scandinavia through Novgorod and down the Dnieper River to Kiev, the Black Sea and Constantinople. Russia was in touch with the rich cosmopolitan civilization of the Eastern Empire and, at the time when William the Conqueror was reorganizing his kingdom in England, Yaroslav the Wise was building great churches in Kiev, and Yuri Dolgoruki establishing the first city on the high banks of the Moscow River, a wooden palisaded fortress that, from the early sketches, shows an uncanny resemblance to the pictures of Hochelaga that Jacques Cartier has left to us. The principalities of Southern Russia, based on Kiev, and those of Northern Russia, based on Vladimir and Moscow, enjoyed centuries of prosperity until the Golden Horde of the Tartars swept out of Mongolia and destroyed their cities. The ruins of the Golden Gates of Kiev are mute testimony to that conquest.

Until the Moscovy Company of England re-established contact with Moscow, by way of Archangel, in the reign of Queen Elizabeth I, western Europe had no real knowledge of Russia, and it was not until Peter the Great, setting out to westernize his empire, established his new capital at what is now Leningrad that contact was really resumed. But difficulties of language and the Cyrillic alphabet have always been barriers to full understanding between Russia and the West. From the time of Peter the Great onwards all Russian officials, and most of the aristocracy, spoke French. Many also spoke English. The rest of the world tended to rely upon these groups for its information and few people from the West took the trouble to learn Russian so that they might form their own independent opinions.

Since the seventeenth century, moreover, the history of Russia resembles in many ways that of North America. Transportation was the key to the opening up of great territories. The construction of the trans-Siberian Railway, the improvement of navigation on the long rivers and, in our own generation, the introduction of jet aeroplanes, have made possible the exploration and exploitation of vast areas untouched since the beginning of time. The utilization of the great forests of central Siberia, and of the tremendous mineral resources of that region, is similar in its general pattern to the development of the Canadian northland, while the construction of dams and powerhouses to provide steadily increasing quantities of hydro-electric energy intensifies the similarity. Russia has expanded eastward to exploit its hinterland in the same way that Canada has expanded westward, and the great farms of "the new lands" recall to the mind of the Canadian traveller our own western Prairies. Human energy, armed with new scientific and technical power, is revolutionizing the economy of both countries in parallel fashion.

This pattern of expansion has been intensified since the end of the Second World War, but it began a century ago. It was the old Czarist government of Russia, in the nineteenth century, that spread out into Georgia, Armenia, Uzbekistan and Turkestan, so that the geographical pattern of modern Russia, except for its Baltic Republics and its European satellite states, was laid down long before Karl Marx was born. The dynamic peoples who inhabit this great area are moving ahead rapidly. Their standard of living today is much below that of North America, but more significance attaches to the fact that it is improving rapidly.

TABLE I

THE EXPANDING PRODUCTION OF THE U.S.S.R.

		1928	1940	1950	1955
I.	**POPULATION**				
	Population of the U.S.S.R. within present geographic boundaries (millions)	147	192	200*	204*
II.	**THE OUTPUT OF PRODUCER GOODS**				
	Pig iron (millions of tons)	3	15	19	33
	Coal (millions of tons)	36	166	261	391
	Oil (millions of tons)	12	31	38	71
	Gas (millions of cubic metres)	331	3,388	6,180	10,355
	Electric power (billions of Kwh)	1	5	13	23
	Chemical fertilizers (thousands of tons)	135	3,022	5,492	9,629
	Metal cutting lathes (in thousands)	2	58	70	118
	Automobiles (thousands)	1	145	363	445
	Tractors (thousands of units	1	32	109	163
	in terms of 15 h.p. units)	2	66	241	322
	Bulldozers (units)	—	118	3,778	7,497
	Spinning machines	66	1,109	1,958	1,990
	Looms (units)	3,700	1,800	8,700	16,000
	Sawn timber (millions of cubic metres)	36	118	161	214
	Cement (millions of tons)	2	6	10	23
	Bricks (millions of units)	3	8	10	21
III.	**THE OUTPUT OF CONSUMER GOODS**				
	Clothing				
	Cotton fabrics (millions of metres)	2,678	3,954	3,899	5,904
	Woolen fabrics (millions of metres)	87	120	155	251
	Silk fabrics (millions of metres)	10	77	130	526
	Synthetic fibres (thousands of tons)	—	11	24	111
	Socks and stockings (millions of pairs)	68	485	472	772
	Leather footwear (millions of pairs)	58	211	203	275
	Household appliances				
	Wireless and TV sets (in thousands)	—	161	1,083	4,024
	Refrigerators (in thousands)	—	4	1	152
	Washing machines (in thousands)	—	—	—	87
	Sewing machines (in thousands)	286	175	502	1,611
	Cameras (in thousands)	—	355	260	1,023
	Gramophones (in thousands)	—	314	367	848

11

TABLE I (cont'd)

	1928	1940	1950	1955
Food				
Granulated sugar (thousands of tons)	1,283	2,151	2,523	3,419
Meat (thousands of tons)	678	1,501	1,556	2,522
Fish (thousands of tons)	840	1,404	1,755	2,740
Butter (thousands of tons)	82	226	336	459
Canned goods (millions of cans)	125	1,113	1,535	3,223
Confectionery (thousands of tons)	99	790	993	1,382
Housing				
Total floor space (in millions of square metres) of new housing projects completed during the year	7.5*	10.0*	24.2	32.3
New hospitals and clinics (thousands of beds)	—	3.4	11.0	14.6

*These figures are approximations.

The figures[1] in Table I indicate that although the output of producer goods expanded much earlier and more steadily, the supply of consumer goods in 1950 (when related to the growth of population) shows very little improvement in the standard of living over a twenty-year period. Against that comparative stagnation, the improvement between 1950 and 1955 is dramatic and all the evidence suggests that the figures for subsequent years, when they become available, will show a continuation of this trend.

Gross national product in the U.S.S.R. is increasing at an annual rate greater than that of Canada or the United States, and by 1970 or 1975 Russia expects to attain a standard of living equal to ours. Even today, Russian science and technology are not inferior to our own—as Sputnik has demon-

[1]These statistics are taken from *National Economy of the U.S.S.R.: Statistical Returns, Moscow, 1957*, which is a most valuable statistical abstract. Experts agree that the information now being published by the Soviet government is both more comprehensive and more accurate than was the case a decade ago. Most of the information in Table I is to be found on pages 17, 144, 145 and 146 of the above-mentioned book.

strated—and the government of the U.S.S.R. is doing its best to attain, and maintain, world leadership in these fields.

It is imperative, then, that we should learn all that we can about the U.S.S.R. in order to understand its people—their habits, their ambitions and their thoughts. Without deeper knowledge than we now possess we cannot hope to formulate wise policies; and if we are unwise, our children will pay for our mistakes.

2. Universities, Colleges, and Research Institutes

ALTHOUGH THERE ARE FIFTEEN REPUBLICS INCLUDED IN THE federation of the U.S.S.R.—some of them with a separate language of their own and an indigenous cultural tradition—the federal government in Moscow has the final responsibility for the development of higher education, by which I mean all educational and research institutions that admit students who have satisfactorily completed the programme of the ten-year schools. As is the case in England or in France today, the pattern of education and its quality is more or less the same throughout the country. It matters little whether one is discussing Moscow or Central Siberia. In this sense Russia is definitely European in pattern rather than North American.[1]

Responsibility is not, however, centralized in a single Moscow ministry, as the classification in Table II clearly indicates. Many of the most outstanding postgraduate research

[1]*Scientist in Russia* by Sir Eric Ashby (Pelican Books, London, 1947) is still the most useful introduction to this aspect of Russian life. *Soviet Education for Science and Technology* by Dr. Alexander G. Korol (New York, 1957) is also valuable, while the recently published *Cultural Progress in the U.S.S.R.* (Moscow, 1958) contains important statistical information. All of the information contained in the statistical tables in this, and subsequent, chapters is derived from this source or from the *National Economy of the U.S.S.R.* previously mentioned.

14

TABLE II

DISTRIBUTION OF TEACHERS AND RESEARCH WORKERS AMONG THE VARIOUS
TYPES OF HIGHER EDUCATIONAL INSTITUTIONS IN THE U.S.S.R.,
OCTOBER 1, 1955

	Total number	U.S.S.R. Academy of Sciences	Academies of Science of Union Republics	Other scientific institutions	Higher educational establishments	At enterprise establishments and in administrative staffs*
Total number of individuals	223,893	13,009	7,993	75,509	119,059	8,323
Those with scientific degree of Doctor of Science	9,460	1,317	484	1,727	5,547	385
Including those with scientific title of:						
Professor	7,589	753	375	1,169	5,070	222
Senior Research Worker	1,010	510	76	365	37	22
Those with scientific degree of Candidate of Science	77,961	4,975	3,826	18,797	43,450	6,913
Including those with scientific title of:						
Professor	503	18	11	88	342	44
Senior Research Worker	12,928	1,996	1,477	8,279	647	529
Assistant Professor	25,018	154	245	1,054	22,500	1,065
Junior Research Worker	2,198	255	429	1,399	73	42
Assistant	2,045	10	3	54	1,791	187
Those without scientific degree but with scientific title	17,490	529	854	7,551	7,531	1,025
Professor	875	3	4	55	717	96
Senior Research Worker	657	56	15	446	64	76
Assistant Professor	3,080	5	12	90	2,580	393
Junior Research Worker	8,744	460	820	6,917	244	303
Assistant	4,134	5	3	43	3,926	157

*Only those with a scientific degree or title.

15

institutes are supervised by the Academy of Sciences of the U.S.S.R. which has on its payroll more than 5 per cent of all the scholars and scientists[2] included in the Table. This organization, although it receives its tremendous budget from the central government, is theoretically (and to a very large extent in practice) independent of the government. In a sense, the Academy of Sciences resembles the Royal Society of Canada. It is a self-perpetuating body that came into existence in 1725 under the patronage of Peter the Great, with Lomonosov as its first President, in which the Members —themselves eminent scholars elected for that reason in the past—elect from time to time the most outstanding scholars of the coming generation.[3] Election is for life, as in the case of the Royal Society of Canada, but (unlike the Royal Society) each member receives a substantial salary and—as has been said—the Academy as a whole administers a budget of thousands of millions of roubles a year, which is provided from the revenues of the central government in Moscow.

Much the same comments could be made in regard to the Academies of the separate Republics, which include on their aggregate payrolls approximately 3 per cent of all the scientists in the U.S.S.R. It should, moreover, be emphasized, since this fact has caused misunderstanding in the West, that the word "science" in Russia embraces all knowledge. The Academies of Science include (as does the Royal Society of Canada) history, philosophy, languages and literature in

[2]To avoid confusion, it must be remembered that the Russian use of the word "scientist" includes scholars in all fields. The Russian use of the word "research worker" also includes all university teachers and all teachers in other institutions of higher education.

[3]Sir Eric Ashby points out that "Elections to the Academy are made by the votes of Academicians on the recommendation of expert committees. . . . Nearly all Academicians are first-class scientists. . . . Politics plays a very minor part in the elections. Here and there a man has been elected to the Academy on political rather than intellectual merit . . . but these egregious exceptions do not seriously weaken the imposing intellectual strength of the Academy." *Scientist in Russia*, pp. 20–1.

their membership, as well as chemistry, geology and physics. When a Russian talks of the sciences he is not contrasting them with the humanities. The term includes both.

In addition to the institutes that are sponsored by the Academy, there are Institutes of Pedagogy that are under the Ministry of Education and Institutes of Medicine and Dentistry that derive their budgets from the Ministry of Health. There are no medical schools in Russian universities. The Institutes of Agriculture are, naturally, the responsibility of the Ministry of Agriculture, while Conservatories of Music and similar colleges in the fields of the fine arts are financed by the Ministry of Culture. In addition to all these, the Ministry of Higher Education is directly responsible for 230 institutions of one kind or another, including the 38 universities that are now in operation in various parts of the U.S.S.R., and more than 50 per cent of all the individuals included in Table II fall within its orbit.

Details of administration, organization and procedure may vary slightly from one supervising authority to another, but on an average the institutions of higher education obtain 99 per cent of their operating revenues and capital funds for new construction from the Ministry to which they are responsible, or from the Academy of Sciences, that is from the aggregate revenues of the central government of the U.S.S.R. The remaining revenue comes from industrial research grants. In each case the Rector of the University or Institute presents his budget requests to the appropriate Ministry in Moscow, in the same way that provincial universities in Canada present their requests to the provincial governments. University Rectors and Directors of Institutes insisted, on many different occasions, that they never got quite as much money from the government as they would like to have (which sounded very much like some of the comparable comments that I heard from Canadian colleagues at recent meetings of the National Conference of Canadian Universities and Colleges in Saskatoon). Each of them insisted, however, that all requests that were really essential, and supported by adequate arguments, were granted by the central authority—and to a Canadian observer the size of the university budgets, in proportion to student enrolment, were generous enough to make one's mouth water.

The most important section of the budget for any university administrator anywhere in the world is that which provides the money for the salaries of the teaching staff—and in this area the U.S.S.R., in spite of its Communist philosophy, has adopted the basic principles of capitalism. The Russians are profoundly convinced of the need for larger numbers of highly trained men and women, not only in the physical sciences and technology but in all the fields of culture and the humanities. To develop the best possible educational system, they want to attract to the staffs of the universities and the other institutes the ablest men and women from all parts of the country. To attract these men and women they offer salaries that are higher than those paid by industry or by government for comparable talent. It is as simple as that, an application of the basic philosophy of capitalism as it has operated in Canada and the United States whenever we really wanted men and women of outstanding capacity to develop our natural resources and prosper our economy.

Comparisons between dollars and roubles are difficult in terms of cost of living. The official exchange rate is R4 = $1, which certainly over-values the rouble in terms of relative costs of living. My own estimate, arrived at after a good deal of discussion with economists in Moscow, is that five or six roubles in Russia is about equal to one dollar in Canada, in terms of internal purchasing power for a typical family in the respective countries, after deduction of income tax. This latter point is important because there is no tax on low in-

18

comes in the U.S.S.R., and the maximum tax, which is levied on those in, let us say, the top 5 per cent of the income brackets (roughly R3000 per month or over) is 13 per cent. If all goes well economically, the U.S.S.R. plans to abolish all income taxes in 1960.

More significant than the comparison with Canadian salaries is the comparison with other incomes in the U.S.S.R. At the bottom of the scale, unskilled labour will earn R250 to R350 per month, and since the minimum income for comfortable middle-class living for a family of four is about R2000 per month, this means that more than one member of the family that wishes to raise its standard of living is likely to seek gainful employment. In the U.S.S.R. women are encouraged to work, as are young people who have graduated from school, and one must think of family income (rather than individual income) in appraising the standard of living.

At a higher level, physicians immediately after leaving medical school will receive about R800 per month and—unless they become professors or eminent research workers—are unlikely to rise to more than R3000 per month at any stage in their careers. School teachers start at R800 per month, and the best of them may rise to R2000, while the same range (or a little higher) is appropriate for highly skilled workers on farms or in factories. Deputy ministers in government service in Moscow receive about R5000 per month, with slightly more for some of the most important and senior among them.

Against this background of comparison, consider the case of the university teacher, whether he is on the staff of old universities like Moscow and Leningrad or new institutions in Central Asia or Siberia. As a graduate student he will get some R1500 per month for part-time work as an assistant. The best of the graduate students, as they approach the final stages of the doctorate, will be appointed docent (roughly equivalent to Canadian assistant professors) at R2500, rising to R3500, per month. The best of those who win the doctorate will be promoted to the rank of professor at R4500 per month which, if they become department chairmen, is raised to R5500 per month.

TABLE III

DISTRIBUTION BY RANK OF SCHOLARS AND SCIENTISTS IN THE U.S.S.R.
(in thousands)

	1947	1950	1955
Total number of research workers	145.6	162.5	223.9
in scientific institutions	59.3	70.5	96.5
in higher educational establishments	81.5	86.5	119.1
at enterprise establishments, and in			
administrative staffs*	4.8	5.5	8.3
Those with scientific degree of			
Doctor of Science	7.7	8.3	9.5
Candidate of Science	36.9	45.5	78.0
Those with scientific title of			
Professor**	8.9	8.9	9.0
Assistant Professor	20.2	21.8	28.6
Senior Research Worker	9.8	11.4	14.6
Junior Research Worker and Assistant	25.6	19.6	17.1
women	51.3	59.0	81.6
members and candidate members of the			
Communist Party	53.8	64.8	96.8

*Only those with a scientific degree or title.
**Inclusive of Members and Corresponding Members of Academies of Sciences.

NOTE: In 1913 there were a little more than 10,000 research workers in scientific institutions and higher educational establishments; in 1940, 98,300 persons.

These are generous salaries, but it should be remembered that the number of individuals who attain this comfort and prestige is not large. Out of a total U.S.S.R. population of more than 200,000,000 there were, in 1955, 9,000 professors (as shown in Table III) and 28,600 people who held a rank equivalent to assistant professor. Candidates approaching the doctorate and aspiring to these positions numbered 78,000.

20

Even though the number of individuals may not be large in proportion to population, the financial advantage accruing to them is greater than these figures of basic salary indicate. If a man is elected to membership in the Academy of Sciences—as outstanding professors often are—he receives a supplementary income of R5,000 per month, that is, a total of R10,500 if he is department chairman at his university, as is frequently the case. This supplementary stipend to Academicians, by the way, continues after retirement from active teaching or research, and only terminates at death.

Whether he be Academician, or an eager young man who has not yet attained that eminence, the professor can supplement his income in various ways. Like his Canadian counterpart, the professor of economics, science or engineering can engage in consultation for government departments or for industrial enterprises. This has become so popular in Russia that the Ministry of Higher Education has had to establish some limit on outside activity and, at present, the maximum additional income that a professor may earn from consultation work of this kind is one-half of his basic university salary.

Even within the university itself, however, there are additional sources of revenue for the able and energetic professor. If he (or she, since many women hold the rank of professor) writes a book, he receives a bonus of R3000 for each "sheet," that is, 16 printed pages. This is a lump-sum payment, since there are no annual royalties on these publications, but one eminent Professor of English Literature, who has published several textbooks and critical studies, told me that she customarily earned R50,000 to R60,000 a year from this source alone. There is, moreover, in the budget of each university a fund at the disposal of the Rector and the Academic Council[4]

4Although the Academic Council, like the Senate at most Canadian universities, includes representatives of the university administration and elected representatives of the various faculties, it differs in the fact that it also includes official representatives of the Communist party as well as representatives of the University Trade Unions, whose membership is made up largely of students.

(a body comparable in many ways to the Senate at Canadian universities) for tax-free awards to members of the teaching staff who have done outstanding work during the session. The arrangements vary in detail from one university to another, as we might expect, but at the Lomonosov University in Moscow (the largest in the U.S.S.R. at the moment) this fund amounts to 3 per cent of the total budget of R300 millions, that is, R9,000,000 a year. The awards made to individual members of the staff during recent years range from a minimum of R500 to a maximum of R100,000—the latter going to men who had made outstanding discoveries as a result of their researches or, in the case of technology, really significant inventions.

Is it surprising that the ablest and most ambitious men and women in the U.S.S.R. want to be professors? This is not due to Communism, and the majority of university teachers (like the majority of all people in Russia) are not active members of the Communist party. All professors are, however, in the top one per cent of incomes in the U.S.S.R., and their incomes purchase comfortable housing, automobiles, personal servants, good clothes, and all the other comforts of life. The "teaching load" of a professor, moreover, is not onerous by Canadian standards. He is expected to teach not less than four, nor more than eight hours each week, in addition to supervising graduate students, and the exact programme (as in Canada) is determined in the light of his research activities, on the one hand, and his administrative responsibilities on the other.

On the other side of the medal, there is no such thing as academic tenure, and nobody has thought of creating a Russian Association of University Teachers to attain, let alone to defend, that ideal. Academic appointments may be reviewed at any time by the Department Chairman, the Dean, the Rector or the Ministry of Higher Education, and there is

22

no question that a man who proved himself incompetent would receive short shrift. There is in fact a requirement, as in the case of many Canadian university teachers up to the rank of associate professor, that the appointment must be reviewed once every five years, but my impression is that this review is little more than a formality in the case of a man who is doing good work—as it is in Canada. Many of the university professors with whom I talked had held their positions for much longer than five years—some of them for more than thirty—and, although they discussed at length many other problems and frustrations connected with their work, not one of them suggested any personal concern with insecurity of tenure. To many Canadians such a pattern of appointment would seem most unsatisfactory, and for the past year Canada has been treated to extensive discussions of academic tenure, from all sides, in regard to the affairs of the United College in Winnipeg. I think however that the Russian professors are sincere in their insistence that this problem —if it be one—does not worry them.

Two supplementary questions have been raised on many occasions since this article was first published. Are the professors in the fields that we in Canada label the humanities as generously treated as those in the physical sciences? What is the relative importance in higher education of the universities on the one hand and of the specialized institutes on the other?

The answer to the second question is statistically stated in Table IV. If we measure importance by the total number of undergraduate students, the universities account for rather less than one-tenth of the total figure and the ratio is constant from 1940 to 1955. If, on the other hand, we think in terms of postgraduate students—the men and women who continue their studies beyond the first university diploma but (in the

Russian classification) have not yet qualified as Candidates—it is apparent that the universities were in 1955 responsible for two-thirds of the total. We should not, however, overlook the fact that the work of the institutes in this field has expanded fourfold during the period from 1940 to 1950 so that the relative importance of the universities in postgraduate work is clearly declining in spite of the steady increase in the number of students.

TABLE IV

THE RELATIVE IMPORTANCE OF UNIVERSITIES IN THE FIELD OF
HIGHER EDUCATION IN THE U.S.S.R.

	1940–1	1950–1	1955–6
Number of institutions of higher education	917	880	765
Total number of undergraduate students			
(including correspondence students)	811,700	1,247,400	1,867,000
Number of students graduating	126,100	176,900	245,800
Number of universities	29	33	33
Total number of undergraduate students			
(including correspondence students)	75,682	108,737	166,256
Number of students in the first year	22,334	27,127	36,690
Number of students graduating	7,963	15,626	22,362
Total number of postgraduate students	16,900	19,400	29,362
In universities and teaching institutions	13,200	10,700	16,774
In research institutes	3,700	8,700	12,588

The question regarding relative treatment of the humanities and the physical sciences in the U.S.S.R. is harder to answer. In the first place, there is the difficulty of applying to Russian educational statistics a classification that Russia does not recognize. Not everyone will agree with the classification that I have made in Tables V and VI—and I must admit that architecture and geography (both of which include some knowledge of the physical sciences and technology) are included as social sciences simply because the available data do not permit a more accurate breakdown.

In spite of these question-marks, the figures are interesting.

TABLE V
DISTRIBUTION OF POSTGRADUATE STUDENTS, IN 1956,
BY SUBJECT AND TYPE OF INSTITUTION

	Total number	Number in universities & teaching institutes	Number in research institutes
Humanities and social sciences			
Philology and languages	2,164	1,736	428
History and philosophy	2,064	1,432	632
Economics	1,810	1,295	515
Pedagogy	1,037	765	272
Art	430	333	97
Law	367	274	93
Geography	359	212	147
Architecture	186	78	108
	8,417	6,125	2,292
Medical and biological sciences			
Agriculture and veterinary	2,564	910	1,654
Medicine and pharmacy	2,164	1,624	540
Biology	1,426	583	843
	6,154	3,117	3,037
Physical sciences and technology			
Engineering	9,358	4,562	4,796
Physics and mathematics	2,855	1,983	872
Chemistry	1,318	483	835
Geology and mineralogy	1,260	504	756
	14,791	7,532	7,259
GRAND TOTAL	29,362	16,774	12,588

Almost one-third of all the postgraduate students in the
U.S.S.R. are specializing in the humanities or the social
sciences, and the predominant fields of interest are languages,
history and philosophy (presumably Communist), economics
and pedagogy. It is also worthy of note that three-quarters
of these graduate students are at the universities, whereas in
the medical and physical sciences at least half of the graduate
students are working at research institutes outside the university.

25

TABLE VI

DISTRIBUTION OF UNIVERSITY TEACHERS AND RESEARCH WORKERS
BY FIELDS OF SPECIALIZATION, U.S.S.R., 1955

	Total number of teachers	Number of Doctors of Science	Number who are Candidates of Science
Humanities and social sciences			
Philology and languages	17,743	248	4,062
History and philosophy	15,305	325	6,987
Pedagogy	11,478	74	1,923
Economics	8,247	203	3,762
Art	4,000	81	617
Geography	3,381	144	1,347
Law	1,607	91	1,027
Architecture	876	31	376
	62,637	1,197	20,101
Medical and biological sciences			
Medical and pharmaceutical	25,326	2,275	12,436
Agriculture and veterinary science	15,135	736	6,021
Biology	11,009	946	5,544
	51,470	4,457	24,001
Physical sciences and technology			
Engineering	61,107	1,855	20,653
Physics and mathematics	20,077	825	5,364
Chemistry	16,435	626	4,639
Geology and mineralogy	5,653	480	2,262
	103,272	3,786	32,918
Miscellaneous (not classified)	6,514	20	941
GRAND TOTAL	223,890	9,460	77,961

These figures are reassuring, but those in Table VI raise
new doubts. No figures are available to show the number of
professors or Academicians in each of the fields, but the
ratio between the total number of teachers and the number
that hold the degree of Doctor of Science—a high academic
rank in the U.S.S.R.—is interesting. In the fields of the
humanities and the social sciences, less than 2 per cent of
the teachers are Doctors of Science; less than 33 per cent
are candidates who might expect soon to win that degree.

In the medical and biological sciences, the comparable figures are 8 per cent and 45 per cent; in the physical sciences and technology 3 per cent and 31 per cent. It would seem therefore that senior rank and the accompanying high emolument are less easily won by humanists and social scientists than by their academic brethren in other fields. The differences within each of the broad classifications are also interesting, ranging from a low in pedagogy to the abnormally high ratio found in the medical and pharmaceutical sciences.

3. The University Student

DURING THE PAST THIRTY YEARS THE U.S.S.R. HAS DEVOTED great attention to the development of its schools. The figures in Table VII are worth pondering. The increase in the total number of children attending school, from 11,368,678 in 1927 to 28,100,704 in 1955 (the last year for which statistics are available) is dramatic enough, but the increase in the number of pupils attending the senior grades of what, in Canada, we should call high school is staggering. During the five years from 1950 to 1955 the number has quadrupled, growing from 1,495,981 to 5,253,070.

Each boy or girl who satisfactorily completes the tenth year of school (under the plan in effect until 1959) is eligible to take the university entrance examination and, if successful, to go to college. There is, however, no compulsion to continue his or her education at university or at one of the many institutes that have already been mentioned. He, or she, will be sixteen or seventeen years of age, and able to seek a job in industry, in the civil service or on one of the collective farms.

The U.S.S.R. is, however, anxious to encourage all lads and lasses of outstanding ability to attain higher educational qualifications and the policy that is followed is similar, in its

28

TABLE VII

THE EXPANSION OF REGULAR SCHOOL FACILITIES
IN THE U.S.S.R.

	1927–8	1940–1	1950–1	1955–6
Population of U.S.S.R. (millions)	147	192	200	204
Number of schools				
Primary	114,401	191,545	126,426	109,756
Seven-year	6,554	45,745	59,640	58,739
Secondary	1,775	18,811	14,961	26,863
Others	1,449	1,095	601	913
Total	118,558	257,196	201,628	195,271*
Number of pupils				
In Grades 1–4	9,910,407	21,375,172	19,670,796	13,579,460
In Grades 5–7	1,437,522	10,767,360	12,031,146	9,268,174
In Grades 8–10 (+ 11)	126,625	2,367,734	1,495,981	5,253,070
Total	11,368,678	35,510,266	33,197,923	28,100,704
Number of teachers	346,493	1,215,967	1,433,401	1,655,164

*Because the demand for education has outrun the construction of new schools, 101,003 of these schools operated on a two-shift basis in 1955–6, while 1,393 were operating on a three-shift basis.

basic principles, to that by which outstanding scholars and scientists are encouraged to become professors. In the first place, university students are exempt from military service, both during their undergraduate years and after they have graduated. In the second place, a university student from a poor family will probably receive a cash income (by way of scholarship) as high as, or even higher during the two final years, than he could earn in any job likely to be open to him. In the third place, he realizes that a degree or diploma is absolutely essential if he ever wants to attain any of the posts—in industry, government or university life—that carry the highest salaries. High income and high prestige blend to create strong inducement, and a very large proportion of the high school graduates in Russia want to go to college.

How does the ambitious high school graduate attain this goal? The first hurdle is the matriculation examination at the end of his tenth school year, which has already been mentioned. This is a nation-wide examination, identical for all schools in the U.S.S.R., which is set, and marked, by examiners appointed by the Ministry of Higher Education in Moscow, that is, by the Ministry responsible for the universities and not the Ministry of Education under which the schools are operated. It is not a "school-leaving examination," as we know it, but is intended to measure the ability of the individual to enter upon a course of higher education, and heavy emphasis is placed upon the student's command of modern foreign languages, the Russian language, chemistry, mathematics and physics.

The student who fails this examination is automatically excluded from the university. The student who passes must then consider what course he wants to take, and to which university he wishes to apply, since the standard nation-wide examination is acceptable to all universities and other institutions of higher education. These decisions are important because the number of places in the freshman year is nowadays substantially less than the number of applicants. The universities have not expanded as rapidly as the schools and an average for the whole of the U.S.S.R. would seem to be about five applicants for each place in the university. In the institutions that we visited the ratio varied from a low of 3:1 to a high of 50:1, and it is perhaps worth mentioning that the highest ratios were in music and ballet-dancing!

The reasons for this variation are two. In the first place, the government of the U.S.S.R. guarantees a job in his chosen field to every student who satisfactorily completes the university course. To do this, the government must this spring (1959) decide how many chemists, geologists, teachers of

30

English and operatic tenors (to name but a few examples) will be needed in the summer of 1964. This estimate, which is carefully made on the basis of a great deal of data, determines the total number of places in each field of study that will be available for freshmen next autumn at all the institutions of higher education in the U.S.S.R.

In the second place, in determining the exact number of places that will be made available at any one institution, the central government in Moscow is, generally speaking, trying to prevent any substantial increase in the size of the older universities like Moscow (now 22,000 students) and Leningrad (about 12,000 students), and to encourage the growth of newer institutions in the south and east. An applicant of good, but not outstanding, quality therefore has a better chance of admission at the newer universities in Irkutsk or Samarkand but, since all Russian universities (like their Canadian counterparts) want to have a student body of diverse geographical and cultural backgrounds, an outstanding applicant from Turkestan or Armenia will have a better chance of admission to the University of Leningrad than a boy with equal marks whose home is in that city. The problems of the admission office at a Russian university are strangely like those in Canada. Academic grades, geographical residence, health, aptitude and sometimes (although we seldom admit it publicly) the position and aggressiveness of the parents must all be taken into account before deciding which out of the many applicants are to be admitted.

Let us follow the lad who is one of the successful fifth of the applicants. He is admitted to the university of his choice, and embarked on the programme of studies that leads to the diploma which is his goal. The details of the curriculum naturally vary from one subject to another, and it would be tiresome to attempt elaborate comparisons. This information in great detail is available in the official publications of the U.S.S.R.[1]

Some general comments, however, apply to all fields of study—medicine, engineering, music or chemistry. The course usually covers five years, and leads to a diploma that is roughly equivalent to the master's degree at North American universities. During the first three years the student will be expected to attend classes for approximately six hours a day throughout a six-day week, and substantial work is required of him outside classes. The academic session lasts for ten months, with a short break (January 24 to February 6 at the University of Moscow) between the semesters. As to the summer, Mr. Mikryukov is positively eloquent.[2] "The summer vacations last from one and a half to two months, depending on when the student has to do his practical work. The third-year students of the Biology and Soil Science Faculty, for instance, have the shortest vacation, twenty-one days in all, from August 10 to August 31. The Physicists of the fourth year, on the other hand, enjoy the longest summer recess. They take their last exams from the spring semester on June 7–8 and are free until August 10." During this summer vacation, the students are encouraged to relax, "touring the country or at home in their native town, in a rest home or sanatorium (free of charge or at a 70% discount, depending on the means of the student's family), training in a camp for the University's leading sportsmen (also free of charge) or on board ship cruising the country's waterways."

During the last two years of the course the number of classes is sharply reduced, so that the student has more time

[1]A great deal of useful information is also available in Dr. A. G. Korol's *Soviet Education for Science and Technology* (New York, 1957) and in the *Report of Education in the U.S.S.R.* published by the U.S. Office of Education (Washington, 1957, Bulletin 14). Mr. M. Mikryukov's *Students of Moscow University* (Moscow, 1957) although sentimentally exaggerated, also reflects very well the circumstances of student life.

[2] Mikryukov, *Students of Moscow University*, pp. 92–3.

32

for individual study and the preparation of his thesis, but it is quite clear that the Russian student, when he graduates, has done two or three times as much work as the man who graduates with a bachelor's degree at a Canadian university. Conversely, in the professional fields, the Russian student of law or medicine graduates in a shorter period than his Canadian counterpart, since these courses (like all the others) take no more than five years from matriculation.

The required courses—required in all faculties at all institutions—must once again be mentioned. No matter what his specialty, our student must take a course in "The History of the Party" in each of the first two years, a course on political economy in the third year, on dialectical materialism in the fourth and on historical materialism in his final year. In order to graduate, at the end of the five years, the student must pass comprehensive examinations in his special subject (for example, physics) which are set by the university, and a series of examinations set by the Ministry of Higher Education, for the whole country, on the required subjects above. He must also write a thesis in his special subject, and defend it publicly before the faculty and the senior students.

This is a stiff academic programme, but if the student has to work hard he also enjoys several advantages over his contemporaries who did not gain admission to university. First of all, there are no tuition fees—no fees of any kind—since education is completely free to those who have the ability and the strength of character to undertake it. Secondly, as I have said earlier, the student is exempt from the call-up for three years of military service which comes to all other young men on their nineteenth birthday. In the third place, students from all parts of the U.S.S.R. are guaranteed such financial aid as they need to carry on their studies.

More than 80 per cent of all the students now enrolled at institutions of higher education in the U.S.S.R. receive stipends—the Russian term that covers both scholarships and bursaries. At the Lomonosov University in Moscow, 85 per cent of the students are in receipt of stipends this year; at Leningrad, 82 per cent; at Kiev, 90 per cent; at the Institute of Foreign Languages (where there are many young women students from well-to-do families), 60 per cent. For the country as a whole, approximately 25 per cent of the total university budget is allocated for the payment of such stipends.

The precise amount of the individual stipend varies widely, being determined in each case (usually by a joint committee of students and faculty) on the basis of both financial need and academic performance. If the grades of the student fall to C he is apt to lose the stipend until his grades improve; if he maintains an A average the stipend is increased by 25 per cent and, for the most brilliant students in the last two years, there are a few princely awards of as much as R1000 per month. The typical range of stipends would, however, be from R250 to R500 per month—subject to 25 per cent increase for A grades—and this compares favourably with the wages that the student would be likely to earn if he left college and went out to find a job! Good students in the last two years, when the load of academic courses is lighter, may also get appointments as part-time laboratory assistants which pay approximately R450 per month in addition to their stipends. These stipends are paid for all twelve months so that the student may have money for his summer holiday as well as for his living expenses during the academic session.

For out-of-town students, moreover, there are hostels at all Russian universities and student cafeterias where good meals can be purchased at comparatively low prices. The quality of the hostel accommodation varies enormously. In the magnificent new buildings of the Lomonosov University in Moscow—the showpiece of Russian higher education—the best accommodation is as good as that at any Canadian university, and better than some. At Kiev, which is still in the process of rebuilding after the devastation of the Second World War, many of the hostels are old private houses where five, six or seven students share a room. But, in spite of the differences in quality, all of the hostels are amazingly cheap. In the places that we visited the rates ranged from R10 per month in Kiev to R30 per month in Moscow, low in comparison either to the student stipends or to the rates that students have to pay for university residences or boarding houses in North America.

It should be pointed out, moreover, that at all Russian universities students from foreign countries are eligible for stipends and for accommodation in the hostels on the same basis as students from the U.S.S.R. We met and talked with students from China, India, Indonesia and other parts of Southeast Asia, as well as exchange students from Great Britain and the United States. Most of them, as one might expect, are at Moscow or Leningrad, but each university in the U.S.S.R. is eager to attract students from foreign countries, recognizing that a significant part of the process of education is the impact of students upon each other. The student from a foreign country, like the student from a distant part of the U.S.S.R., often has a better chance of admission, and perhaps a more generous stipend, than the student from the city in which the university is situated.

Quite clearly, students and professors constitute a privileged class in the U.S.S.R. More educated men and women are needed by the country, and the government is willing to offer the inducements that will attract the best brains in the country.

4. The Relation of Education to Life

STUDENTS ARE A PRIVILEGED CLASS IN THE U.S.S.R., AND ON September 21, 1958, it was announced that Mr. Nikita Khrushchev had sent to the Central Committee a memorandum expressing his fear that this privileged class was losing touch with the realities of life—with the toil of the farm and the skilled craftsmanship of the factory worker. To avoid the schism in society, and prevent the development of a "white collar" intelligentsia, Mr. Khrushchev bluntly proposed that youngsters should go to work after eight years of school and complete their education by correspondence, mostly in their spare time. No student should be admitted to university unless he had at least two years' experience of employment and could produce satisfactory reports from his employer, the trade union and the Komsomol.

These were far-reaching proposals. Stalin had reformed education to correct the laxity of the earlier pattern and create the system now in existence. Mr. Khrushchev wanted to reform it again to avoid the development of the kind of class consciousness on the part of an educated minority that does not want to dirty its hands, which has bedevilled more than one country in the modern world.

Before discussing the evolution, and implementation, of the Khrushchev reforms, it is necessary to insert a few words of amplification regarding the Russian pattern of higher education. The description in previous articles, for purposes of simplicity, has dealt only with the student who registers at a university or an institute, on a full-time basis, with the intention of completing his work for the diploma in the minimum period of five years. Since the educational reforms of August 29, 1938, however, Russian institutions of higher education have offered two alternative programmes by which the youngster who is, for any reason, unable to register as a full-time student can work for a diploma. If he lives in a city where there is a university he may take evening courses, usually during a period much longer than five years, and then present himself for the same set of comprehensive final examinations that confront the full-time student specializing in his field of interest. For those who live in districts too far from any university to make evening attendance possible, there are in some (but not all) fields of study correspondence courses stretching over an even longer period of years. Correspondence students, like evening students, must at each stage of the course face the standard set of examinations that are taken by regular full-time students so that the ultimate professional qualification of both groups is the same.

It might be assumed, since human nature is pretty much the same all over the world, that most young men and women, if they had the choice, would prefer the more comfortable status of full-time day students to the harder lot of the correspondence student, but the figures in Table VIII show that the total number of evening and extension students

TABLE VIII

GROWTH IN STUDENT ENROLMENT AT INSTITUTIONS OF
HIGHER EDUCATION IN THE U.S.S.R.

	Full-time day students	Evening and correspondence students	Total number of students
1940–1	585,000	226,700	811,700
1950–1	845,100	402,300	1,247,400
1955–6	1,227,900	639,100	1,867,000

has increased more rapidly than the number of full-time students. The explanation is presumably to be found in the limited number of places open to full-time students.

Against this background, we can return to Mr. Khrushchev's proposals of a year ago. When first offered, they elicited a good deal of discussion. The clear merit of giving to all students a closer acquaintance with the practical problems of the economy—with the blood, sweat and tears that lie beneath the statistics—was widely recognized, but several members of the Academy of Sciences and other university leaders pointed out in public speeches that the implementation of the proposal in its crudest form would do irreparable harm. Termination of formal schooling at the eighth year, and the requirement of at least two years in the factory, however valuable in terms of social psychology, might destroy the aptitude for study and would certainly prolong the period required for professional qualification on the part of the student.

This controversy is worth underlining, not only for the intrinsic merit of the arguments but because we in the western world are apt to think that nobody in Russia dares to argue with Mr. Khrushchev, who is both chairman of the Council of Ministers and Secretary of the Communist party! This may have been true during the later years of the period when Stalin held these posts: it is not true today.

38

In due course, during the early days of our stay in the U.S.S.R. Mr. Khrushchev's proposals came before the Supreme Soviet of the R.S.F.S.R., in Moscow, for legislative enactment. Among the members of the Supreme Soviet are several University Rectors (Leningrad and Irkutsk among them) and several members of the Academy of Sciences. The arguments that had been going on in public were repeated, and sharpened, during the course of the debate on the bill, and the legislation that finally emerged differs in several important respects from Mr. Khrushchev's original proposal.

First of all, it has been decided by the Supreme Soviet that the process of familiarizing the child with the practical aspects of modern economic life should begin in the schools in a somewhat different manner. Beginning next September, the ten-year school programme will be spread over eleven years in all except the special schools for musicians and ballet-dancers. No new academic work will be introduced, but the additional time will be used for special programmes designed to help the child to understand the practical problems of agriculture, commerce and industry.

During the eighth and ninth years, that is, at the age of approximately 14 to 16, the pupil will attend special classes, given within the school, on woodwork, metal-work, weaving or agriculture, the exact programme depending on the region of the country and its special interest. These classes are intended to be primarily handicraft classes in which the pupils do things with their own hands, wrestling with the sinewy stubbornness of nature and natural materials. They are not intended to be simple lectures or descriptions.

During the tenth and eleventh years—ages 16 to 18—the pupils will attend school three days a week for regular academic classes. On each of the alternate days they will work for half a day, that is, four hours, in a factory, on a farm, in the courthouse or at a department store (to cite a few examples). The job will be chosen to fit the ultimate ambition of the boy or girl, as closely as is possible in terms of the economic activity in the area surrounding the school. The pupil will be paid for his work at the regular hourly rates for employees with equal skill and experience (or lack of it) and special homework studies will be assigned by the school for the remainder of the day to maintain a lively contact with his academic studies.

This part of the new programme applies to all boys and girls except musicians and dancers, but the proposed pattern of employment after school is finished and the pupil has passed the matriculation examination shows an interesting intellectual precision. In the first place, it has been decided that each university shall have the right in individual cases, at its own discretion, to admit a student who comes directly from school and has no experience of work in farm or factory. The universities expect to use this discretion sparingly—but they have it!

In the second place, the academic members were able to convince the Supreme Soviet that a two-year interruption of study might do irreparable harm to the student of foreign languages, mathematics, theoretical chemistry and theoretical physics. None of these disciplines depends on mature experience of life. Comparatively young people may do outstanding work, and anyone who shows outstanding ability in one of these fields should be encouraged to forge ahead without interruption. It is therefore provided in the new legislation that students of outstanding ability who are qualified to specialize in any one of these four areas shall go directly to university after matriculation. There will be no two-year period of stagnation in gainful employment. The same provision as has been mentioned applies to students of music and ballet dancing, and for the same reasons.

In all other fields, medicine, economics, law, philosophy,

40

engineering and the rest, it is provided that two years of practical employment shall be undertaken before entering university. The interruption of studies is not, however, complete because those who wish to proceed to a university diploma are encouraged during these two years to register for evening or extension courses. If they do so, they are entitled to two months' leave of absence in each calendar year on full pay (provided this does not exceed R1000 a month) in order to study, and to leave of absence with pay, as well as travel expenses when necessary, in order to enable them to go to the university to sit the examinations set for full-time day students in each of the subjects. Any student who satisfactorily completes two years of evening or extension work under this scheme, and passes the examinations set by the university for full-time students at the end of their first year, will become eligible to enter the second year of the course as a full-time student and to attain his diploma after four further years of full-time study.

The new *Law on Strengthening the Ties of the School with Life and Further Developing the System of Public Education* recognizes, however, that the number of places for full-time students will always be limited. Not all of those who complete the first two years of correspondence work will gain admission. Elaborate provision is therefore made to encourage them to continue as correspondence students. During the third, and subsequent, years of such a programme the student will be entitled to three months' leave of absence with pay, and when he has to prepare and defend his thesis in the final year this is increased to four months. The wage or salary received by each individual during these "study-leaves" shall be the average of his monthly earnings during the preceding twelve months, but shall not in any case exceed R1000 per month. It is further provided that in the final year of the course the student, if he so desires, may have an additional day off each week for studying, but shall only receive half pay for this extra time.

It as an interesting experiment, only possible in a country where the government owns all the means of production and can therefore make plans which, even if they help the student, will create headaches for those who have to administer farms, factories and offices. One could argue as long, and as warmly, as the Russians have argued about it, but those of us who remember the splendid maturity of the Canadian veterans who came back to college after the last war have a strong suspicion that a little "experience of life" between school and college may not be a bad thing. We can also notice, as an important and interesting fact, the way in which a proposal made by Mr. Khrushchev as chief of the government at Moscow has been hammered out, and reshaped in parliamentary debate, to create a programme which, however much one may like or dislike some of its details, is a logical and defensible experiment in the field of higher education.

5. The Cultural Pleasures of Life

A RECENT STUDY BY MR. RICHARD FINDLATER ON *The Future of the Theatre* (in England) points out that the living theatre is likely to die unless there is greater support from the government for a national theatre, assistance in the construction of playhouses in smaller towns and more funds for the Arts Council. Since Sir Henry Irving died in 1905, 500 British theatres have gone out of existence: only 200 remain. Outside of London, as recently as 1950, there were 140 theatrical touring companies in the United Kingdom: today there are 55. *Country Life*, in commenting on the report, suggests that a rising actor in England is lucky nowadays if he gets ten roles a year, whereas Irving played 400 in three years during his apprenticeship. "It seems certain that the days of private enterprise in the theatre, if it is to survive as an art, are ending."

If the outlook in England is so gloomy, what of Canada? Any Canadian who has been to London remembers clearly the comparative richness of the offerings of opera, ballet, musical comedy and drama that were available to him. Tens of thousands of Canadians who appreciate these things as an essential part of cultural civilization are supporting the Winnipeg Ballet, La Comédie Canadienne, the Stratford Festivals, a dozen symphony orchestras and similar activities in various parts of Canada; but, even proportionately to population, we have much less than Great Britain.

In these fields of cultural life, the U.S.S.R. offers rich fare to its citzens. Since the Bolshoi Ballet has recently been in Canada, there is no need to comment here on its outstanding performances, but its absence from Moscow during the period of our visit to that city did not greatly reduce the entertainment available to Moscovites. While our party was there we saw *Prince Igor* and *Sadko* brilliantly performed at the Bolshoi Theatre, *Silva* at Comic Opera Theatre, an unforgettable performance of delightful comedy at the Puppet Theatre, *Anna Karenina* at the Moscow Art Theatre (which like the Abbey Theatre in Dublin is one of the great pioneering dramatic organizations that has continued without interruption since the nineteenth century) and a new programme of the Moyschiev Dancers who last year visited Montreal. There was much more to see if we had had more time—and each of these entertainments was available at prices ranging from twenty cents in the gallery to about three or four dollars for the best seats in the house. In each case, moreover, except the puppets and the Moyschiev Dancers, the programme showed at least three names against each character in the ballet, play or opera. Each theatre has, quite literally, a galaxy of stars in its company, and I understand that it is customary for each of them to play no more than five performances a week. Outstanding actors, dancers and singers are paid as much as, but no more than outstanding philosophers, chemists or economists, so that it is quite clear that the Ministry of Culture provides generous financial support.

44

But this, it may be said, is Moscow, the capital of the U.S.S.R. and a great city comparable to London or to New York. The most interesting thing about the U.S.S.R. in this regard was the fact that the performances we saw in much smaller provincial cities were as splendidly staged in opera houses and theatres that were scarcely distinguishable from those in Moscow. (In some respects the Opera House at Tashkent is, in my opinion, the best building of its kind that we visited.) In Leningrad we saw an excellent performance of *Lakmé* that was moving enough to make one forget the "blimpish" stylizing of British officers in India. At Kiev there was *Lohengrin* and *Swan Lake*—the latter with a magnificence that outshone my memories of New York—while the Georgian National Ballet at Tibilisi, in a programme based on local history and legend, provided one of the memorable evenings of our visit. In Tashkent the play was a melodrama about life on a collective farm, but the Uzbek National Theatre and its company were worthy of better things. In every part of the U.S.S.R., as the figures in Table IX eloquently indicate, one finds theatres, opera houses and concert halls—and at each of them a company of actors, dancers and musicians of oustanding ability. At each of them the minimum price of admission is less than that charged for admission to the movies in most Canadian cities, and on each occasion we were impressed by the large number of young people in the audience. On many occasions, undergraduates whom I had met at the university earlier in the day would come up to chat during the intermission.

It should, moreover, be pointed out that in 1953 (the last year for which figures are available) the performances in 190 of these theatres were offered not in Russian but in the local language of the region, and that 36 languages were used during that year.

TABLE IX

Theatrical Entertainment in the U.S.S.R.

| | Number of theatres whose data are referred to | Number of performances | | Number of spectators | | |
		total per annum	per theatre per annum	total per annum (thousand persons)	per theatre per annum (thousand persons)	per one perform-ance
U.S.S.R.						
1950	536	206,833	886	67,977	126.8	329
1953	504	198,309	303	70,851	140.6	357
1954	504	205,461	408	77,220	153.2	376
1955	500	211,634	423	77,960	155.9	368
Opera and ballet theatres	32	11,084	346	8,415	263.0	759
Drama and comedy theatres	347	138,439	399	50,818	146.4	367
Musical comedy theatres	20	7,511	376	4,674	233.7	622
Theatres for children & youth	101	54,600	541	14,053	139.1	257
Theatres in the Union Republics in 1955						
R.S.F.S.R.	280	121,444	434	48,767	174.2	402
Ukrainian S.S.R.	77	36,186	470	12,651	164.3	350
Byelorussian S.S.R.	9	4,087	454	1,537	170.8	376
Usbek S.S.R.	25	9,955	398	2,596	103.9	261
Kazakh S.S.R.	20	7,148	357	1,829	91.4	256
Georgian S.S.R.	20	7,545	373	2,456	122.8	329
Azerbaijan S.S.R.	8	3,003	375	1,260	157.5	420
Lithuanian S.S.R.	8	2,645	331	967	120.8	365
Moldavian S.S.R.	4	1,955	489	537	134.3	275
Latvian S.S.R.	10	4,610	461	1,850	185.0	401
Kirghiz S.S.R.	7	2,609	373	673	96.2	258
Tajik S.S.R.	8	2,344	293	565	70.6	241
Armenian S.S.R.	10	3,034	303	917	91.7	302
Tarkmen S.S.R.	5	1,578	316	336	67.1	213
Estonian S.S.R.	9	3,582	398	1,019	113.3	285

I do not know how many millions of roubles the government spends on all these cultural activities during the course of a year. I do not pretend to know whether it is an appropriate portion of the national budget, in the light of other demands, but quite clearly the Russian government—like those of Italy and France—regards these activities as important. The young Russian, therefore, gets a better opportunity to see first-class living theatre in all its forms than any young North American outside of New York City. Even in New York it is doubtful if young people go as often, for economic reasons.

The organization of entertainment of so high a quality in so many cities requires more than money. It demands talent, and the Ministry of Culture has done its best to see that every youngster with outstanding talent and enthusiasm gets a chance to become an actor, a singer, a dancer, or a musician. The general pattern of application, admission and stipends is closely similar to that for students in physics, chemistry and geology, although in music and dancing the selection takes place at an earlier age and the pupil attends a special school in which his professional studies are integrated into the general curriculum.

In Leningrad, we visited the Aggrippina Habolina Vaganova School of Ballet. It was founded in 1730, the oldest ballet school in the world, and portraits of great dancers from earlier generations adorn its walls, as memory and inspiration. Nadjinsky is among them, and Pavlova. It is probably the best known of all the ballet schools in the U.S.S.R. and its annual budget from the government is R3,500,000. It admits at the age of 10 years (for a nine-year course) outstanding students from every part of the country. There are no fees, and all students who need assistance receive stipends, particularly in the last four years of the course. Last year there were 2,000 applicants for the 60 places in the first year of the course. Out of 60 admitted, experience indicates that approximately 30 will graduate nine years later. One-third of the students are boys and, as we watched class after class at practice, from beginners to the senior class that was almost ready to enter on professional careers, it was apparent that the boys were as enthusiastic as the girls. On each child admitted, the state spends an average of R12,000 a year during the nine-year course—on faculty salaries, on stipends, on the operation of the hostels and on travelling expenses. (When the Leningrad ballet goes on tour, the upper classes at the school go with it, to watch and to gain inspiration.) It is expensive, but the value to society is apparent when one watches the graduates, in theatres all over the U.S.S.R. or on tour in North America, and is delighted by a superb performance.

At Kiev, the capital of the Ukraine, we spent the best part of a day at the Conservatory of Music, of which Professor Pavlichenko is the Rector and Professor Stogarichenko his deputy. Pupils are admitted to the Conservatory only after they have completed the ten-year school course, either at the Musical School which is under the administrative control of the Conservatory (so that musical studies are integrated with the rest of the curriculum) or at some other school. In the latter case, if music has not been adequately taught but the applicant has outstanding ability, the Conservatorium admits him to a two-year preliminary course of intensive preparation.

For the Musical School, applicants are screened at the age of 6 or 7 on the basis of musical talent. All of them receive appropriate stipends from the fifth class onward, that is, after the age of 12, in those cases where family finances make this necessary. No fees are charged for any pupil and all instruments or other necessary equipment are supplied by the school.

The Conservatory of Music itself, like all institutions of higher education, admits only those who have satisfactorily completed the ten-year school, and enrols them for a five-year course leading to the diploma. Any talented student from any part of the U.S.S.R. may apply, and although there are many conservatories in different parts of the U.S.S.R. the applications at Kiev are particularly numerous in the case of singers, since the climate of the Ukraine, like that of Italy, is thought to be conducive to the development of the vocal chords. Last year, in this field, there were fifty times as many applicants as there were places in the freshman class.

At the present time there are 465 full-time students in the Kiev Conservatory and—as an experiment started three years ago—163 extension students who study at home under the direction of teachers approved by the Conservatory. There are also 47 postgraduate students who are looking forward to appointments as teachers rather than as performers.

To teach these students—465 undergraduates and 47 post-graduate students—there are 131 full-time teachers, exclusive of accompanists and secretarial staff. One of these, Professor Revutsky, is a Member of the Academy of Sciences, and twenty are full professors at a salary of R4500 to R5000 per month, as in the case of professors at all institutions of higher education. The docents, like their opposite numbers in physics, philology or economics, receive salaries of R2500 to R3000 per month, so that the total of R8,000,000 a year which constitutes the present budget of the Kiev Conservatory is easy to understand. On an average, the state spends R100,000 on each student during the five years that he (or she) is attending the Conservatory.

When we had finished our discussion with members of the staff, and our visits to some of the classes, the Rector told us that a group of students in the senior class had arranged an impromptu concert for us. I am no musical critic, so that I shall refrain from detailed description of an hour that was sheer delight, but I would like to single out Mr. Kikot, who had a voice that, to my ear, is as good as that of Paul Robeson at his best, and Miss Kudela, who is a splendid soprano. The choice of these two for special mention is not an amateur effort at musical criticism on my part. I mention them for another reason. Miss Kudela lost both of her parents during the war, grew up without schooling, and found employment as an unskilled worker in a textile factory before her voice attracted attention and won her a place in the Conservatory. Mr. Kikot left school at the age of 12 and went to sea as a cabin boy, so that when his voice attracted the attention of the Conservatory it was necessary for special arrangements to be made for him to complete the school curriculum before commencing as an undergraduate. The examples are significant of the effort that is being made in the U.S.S.R. to seek out, and to provide educational opportunities for, all those who have the kind of outstanding talent that will enable them to offer to the world the cultural pleasures of life. Talent is scarce enough in any country: it must not be allowed to go to waste.

6. The Embers of Religion

ON SUNDAY, APRIL 26TH, WE WERE IN TIBILISI, THE CAPITAL of that ancient Kingdom of Georgia to which Christianity was brought by Saint Nina in the fourth century of the Christian era. Not far away in the walled city of Mtsketa, in the Church of the Tree of Life, is the unforgettable Eikon of the wounded Virgin, a beautiful picture of a mother who has known suffering looking tenderly at the babe in her arms and scarcely conscious of the bleeding wound on her right cheek. That wound is a symbol of deep significance. Christianity in Georgia was thrice wounded—by the invading Tartars, again by the Mongols and still again by the conquering hordes of Islam under Suleiman the Magnificent. Three times the Church of the Tree of Life was desecrated and destroyed: three times it was rebuilt and reconsecrated more splendid than before. All the deep memories of fifteen hundred years of triumphant Christianity are recalled by that wound on the cheek of Our Lady of Sorrows.

By the calendar of the Russian Church, April 26, 1959, was Palm Sunday. Lyle Nelson had agreed with me on the previous evening that we should go together and worship on this feast that opens the week which for a Christian has

51

deeper significance than any other in the whole calendar of the year.

The service, we were told, started at nine o'clock, and we decided to go to the Church of Zion—in the heart of Tibilisi —which like the Church of the Tree of Life in the old capital had three times risen in greater strength from devastating defeat and apparent death. Because we did not know the geography of the city we left the hotel soon after eight, with only a map to guide us. There were few people in the streets, and the policeman at the door of the hotel gave us no more than a passing glance. Nobody followed us, nobody paid any attention to us. Twice we lost our way and had to retrace our steps, but at last we found the Church of Zion and entered to join the congregation.

All of the other members of the congregation carried small branches of birch twigs, on which the buds were just opening into the small new leaves that are so vividly and unforgettably green. Two priests, an old man near the altar and a younger priest in the northern transept, were still hearing confession. The rest of the congregation were standing in the nave waiting for the service to begin. The priests retired, and a few minutes later returned in their vestments, and for more than an hour we stood as members of a devout congregation through one of the most moving religious services of my life. When it was over, the older priest gave to each of the worshippers a little loaf of bread—about the size of a large breakfast roll—that had been blessed at the altar, and as the people came out through the porch of the church into the sunshine, carrying their branches of birch leaves and their sanctified bread, they stopped, as churchgoers do everywhere, to chat with their neighbours for a few moments before walking home. At the end of the little street, where it joined a larger thoroughfare, I could see the familiar blue and red uniform of a policeman, but he was busily supervising a queue that was forming outside a pastrycook's shop that was due to open in about half an hour. Neither he, nor anybody else, paid any attention to the little group of worshippers, who had just met in the Church of Zion to celebrate together the two-thousand-year-old memory of Christ's last entry into Jerusalem and to worship God.

Why call such an experience deeply moving? The carrying of birch branches and the distribution of loaves that have been blessed at the altar are, so far as I know, different from the practice of all western churches, but they are not different in spiritual significance from the palms that we carry or the consecrated bread of the communion service. The history of the Church of Zion was old, and the building beautiful, but there are old and beautiful churches in many lands. There are also devout congregations and, by a quirk of memory, I remembered one, on Palm Sunday, 1944, in the little church of St. Mary, Stoke Newington, on the outskirts of London. One shuddered, involuntarily, as two buzz bombs droned across the words of the communion service, exploding not far away, and we emerged at the end of the service into the devastation that earlier bombs had made.

The first reason why the Palm Sunday service in Tibilisi moved me was the simple fact that it was held at all—that the church was there, that priests were attending to the spiritual welfare of their flock, that men and women could come together to worship. We in the western world have heard so much about the suppression of religion in the U.S.S.R., about the famous (or infamous) dictum that religion is no more than the opiate of the masses, that it was significant to find in every part of Russia that we visited open churches in which daily services were conducted for all who wished to attend.

The second, and equally moving, realization was that there were very few such churches and that the congregations were pitifully small. At the Church of Zion, probably because it was Palm Sunday and partly because Georgia is not quite the same as Russia, the congregation was larger than any other that we had seen, but it was pitifully small. Most of the worshippers were women above the age of fifty, many of whom had brought their grand-children. There was a sprinkling of older men, many of them with the erect bearing that suggested army officers of the old school. But we saw scarcely any men or women between the ages of twenty and forty-five. The older generation was continuing the religious habit of a lifetime; they might bring their grandchildren (although we saw most of these, resplendent in new clothes, on Palm Sunday and Easter). The fathers and mothers of those children, and the young people who will soon be fathers and mothers, were conspicuous by their absence. Sunday for them was a holiday, not a holy-day.

The fact that no more than a small minority of the population go to church is underlined by the fact that most of the ancient churches in all the republics that make up the U.S.S.R. are now secular museums under the jurisdiction of the Minister of Culture. Many of them—the ancient cathedrals in the Kremlin, the Cathedral of Saint Isaac at Leningrad, the Sofievsky Cathedral and the Pechersk Lavra at Kiev—are indescribably beautiful. All of them still hold up golden crosses to the sky. All are well cared for and maintained in a condition as good as that in which they were maintained during the old regime, perhaps even better in some cases. On holidays they are thronged with people, most of whom come as curious sightseers, not as worshippers, and there are no priests to minister to them. Even so, I have often seen a man or woman stand quietly before an Eikon or an altar, deep in thought. One cannot penetrate another human mind.

I do not know how many priests there are in Russia today,

but the number must be very much smaller than it once was —and proportionately to population much smaller than in any western country. Most of those that I saw were old men with white beards who had, I should judge, found their vocation before the October Revolution of 1917. Theology is not taught in any university in the U.S.S.R. and although there are a few theological seminaries in various parts of the country for the training of priests the number of ordinands must be pitifully small. I cannot find any statistics.

That little Palm Sunday congregation at the Church of Zion in Tibilisi was deeply moving because one felt that it was a brave relic of ancient days, but in the same breath one felt concern for the days that are still to come. Why has Christianity declined, in one generation of forty years, to so small a band of worshippers in a country which for more than a thousand years—even when large parts of western Europe were still pagan—carried forward the great religious heritage of Constantinople?

No man can dogmatize on this question, but no Christian can fail to think about it in the effort to seek out the answer. We know that the Communist government, after 1917, was anti-clerical. The suppression of the monasteries in Russia under Lenin was no gentler that it had been in England four hundred years earlier in the time of Henry VIII. Although accurate evidence is hard to come by, it seems clear that the Church in Russia was severely persecuted by the Communists for at least a quarter of a century and—even though there are no signs of persecution at present—the calendar of those who suffered martyrdom for the Christian faith must include many Russians whose names, unknown to us in the West and perhaps forgotten by the present generation of their compatriots, are inscribed in the Book of Life.

But if persecution, of itself, were a sufficient answer to the question there would be no Christian Church anywhere in the world. The early Christians endured persecution for nearly three centuries at the hands of Roman authorities who held to an ancient paganism as strongly as the U.S.S.R. holds to Communism, yet the Church emerged from its ordeal stronger than before. Was it not Latimer, at the stake during a later English persecution, who said to his fellow-martyr Ridley "Be of good comfort. We shall this day light such a candle in England as shall never be put out"? John Huss, as the flames rose about him, had the grim courage to make a prophetic pun. "You may burn Huss (goose) now, but Luther (swan) will come!"

Persecution is not the whole answer, nor is the whole answer to be found in the fact that religion is not taught in any school or university in any part of the U.S.S.R. We can find many secular school systems in North America, in France, in England and in other countries, but the existence of secular school systems has not undermined Christianity in those areas. Many men and women, deeply religious, still insist that the teaching of religion is best done in the home and in the church, rather than in schools and colleges supported by the state.

Perhaps the Russian Church, in an earlier generation, was too close to the state and not close enough to the people. The great red-brick fortress walls of the monasteries at Suzdal, among the richest and most beautiful in Old Russia, were not maintained as a protection from invaders but to separate the clergy from the laity. The two thrones in the cathedrals—one for the Czar, the other for the Metropolitan Archbishop— underlined before all men that alliance of church and state which could produce tragic consequences for the church when the state was overthrown in bloody revolution (as it did for a generation in England three hundred years earlier, and still more recently in France).

The ultimate answer must be read in the pages of history

that is yet to be written. We of this generation are too close to the events of the past forty years to appraise accurately their impact on the future but two thousand years of human experience has convinced us that "man shall not live by bread alone." The little Palm Sunday congregation at the Church of Zion, and the even smaller congregaitons in hundreds of other churches in Russia, are facts. They are certainly a legacy of yesterday. Are they a portent for tomorrow?

7. Freedom of Thought?

THE DISCUSSION OF RELIGION IN RUSSIA IN THE PREVIOUS chapter was in terms of Christianity. It must be remembered, however, that the U.S.S.R. includes within its boundaries great numbers of Muslims. There are mosques as far west as Moscow and Leningrad; as one travels southeast through Turkestan and Uzbekistan they greatly outnumber the Christian churches.

The tradition of Islam in these areas is as old as the tradition of Christianity in Kiev and in Moscow. Timur, who lived from 1366 to 1405, had his capital in Samarkand and on his tomb is the simple inscription "The Conqueror of the World." It is not humble, but there is much truth to it. The great Mosque of Bibi Khanum that he built, largest in all the world, was ruined by an earthquake more than sixty years ago, but the smaller mosques—many like those in the Shah Zindeh of exquisite beauty—are no more crowded by worshippers on Friday than are the Christian churches on Sunday. Most of them are now regarded as historical monuments, cared for by the State,[1] but they are not centres of a living

[1]The care of the old mosques is, however, less than that lavished on the old cathedrals. This is not a new phenomenon since Henry Norman (*All the Russias*, p. 333) makes a similar complaint regarding the Czarist government. In my opinion the significant contrast is not between Christian churches and

and lively religion. The Muslim schools that once were found at each of the large mosques—the schools that nurtured the minds of men like Sadriddin Aini, who has left us an unforgettable picture of them in his autobiographical *Pages from My Own Story*—are closed.

Once, long ago, the region that is now Uzbekistan was one of the great centres of human learning and critical thinking. Ulugh-Beg, grandson of Timur, was not only the Governor of Western Turkestan and a great warrior. The remains of the observatory that he built at Samarkand in 1428 recall his eminence as an astronomer. His star catalogue was the first independent study after that of Hipparcus, in Greece, fifteen centuries before him, and even today the astronomical tables that bear his name enjoy a high reputation for accuracy. Is there food for thought in the local legend (not confirmed by the evidence of history!) that he was murdered by religious fanatics in 1449 because they feared that his scientific researches were probing too deeply into the mysteries of God?

Even in the days of Timur and Ulugh-Beg the tradition of critical thought was old in Uzbekistan. Four centuries earlier, in 980, Abu 'Ali Al Hosain Ibn Sina—known to the West as Avicenna—was born near Bokhara. He has well been called the Prince of Physicians, since his Qanun was for 500 years the basic textbook of medicine in both the European and Arabic worlds, but there were more than a hundred other books from his pen. Philosophy, mathematics, economics and music were fascinating fields for his enquiring mind, which illuminated all that it touched upon, so that in the restrospect of history he stands out as one of the great scientists of all time.

---

mosques at the present time but between large centres of population (where the buildings are splendidly maintained) and out-of-the-way places. The Christian monasteries at Suzdal are no better cared for than the Registran in Samarkand.

The Central Asian University, at Tashkent, is today engaged in the task of producing a monumental edition of the works of Avicenna, and scholars in every part of the world are delighted. Here, as in many another case, the publishing houses of the U.S.S.R. are undertaking important tasks—not likely to be profitable in financial terms—that western scholars also like to undertake whenever funds are available.

Great credit is also due to the Central Asian University at Tashkent, and the Alisher Navoi State University at Samarkand, for the tremendous task that they have undertaken in an area where no universities and few schools were in existence as recently as 1920. When the University was established at Tashkent, there were no professors in Russia who understood either Tajik or Uzbek. The staff recruited from the older universities of the U.S.S.R. had to learn the local languages, and not until 1932 was it possible to provide instruction in all subjects in the Uzbek language. During the same period, schools had to be established to teach children, from a population that prior to that time was 85 per cent illiterate, the subjects that they would need for university entrance. Textbooks had to be written in Uzbek and Tajik, or translated from Russian. The present Rector of the Alisher Navoi State University told us proudly that he was the first member of his clan to enter any university; the Rector of the Central Asian University was a member, in 1932, of the first class in that university to receive all their lectures in Uzbek. Today there are 430 members of the teaching staff at Tashkent and 300 in Samarkand, 60 per cent of whom are Uzbeks, and instruction is available in both universities, at the option of the student, in Uzbek, Tadjik or Russian. All of the professors and most of the students are bilingual. Many have command of three or four languages.

This is a tremendous achievement for one generation. It is an unforgettable experience to hear men like Professor

Sadikow—one of the pioneers—describe it, and then to go out of the building and watch the thousands of students (looking much like students in Canada or any western country) walking across the tree-shaded campus from one class to the next. Forty years ago there was no campus here, there were no students—and there were very few modern books in the Uzbek language! The last difficulty is one that no Canadian university has had to face, in spite of the many and difficult problems that each of them has confronted during the past fifty years of rapid growth. One of the things about the U.S.S.R. which provides much food for thought is the confident way in which the central government at Moscow has encouraged the use of local languages in the separate republics, and facilitated the publication of a steadily growing literature in each of these languages. Moscow is so certain that the republics wish to hang together that it has gone out of its way to foster the revival, indeed intense enrichment, of the many independent national cultures that are to be found within the borders of the U.S.S.R. Centralized government has not meant uniformity of culture.

All of this cannot fail to evoke admiration. It is a magnificent job, well done. But one's mind wanders back to Ulugh-Beg and Avicenna. Would a revolutionary scientist, discovering great and fundamental truths of the physical universe that did not accord with current dogma, be elected to membership in the Academy of Sciences today? Or would he meet the fate of that first Ulugh-Beg who looked towards the stars, and understood them, five hundred years ago? What would be the fate of a new Avicenna? It is one thing to publish the works of a great thinker who died nine centuries ago: quite another to put up with the disquieting questions of a man who is not satisfied with the existing order and wants to change it.

These are difficult questions to answer. The critical

thinker, especially in the fields of ethics, politics and economics, is never popular. The Greeks, despite their freedom of thought, condemned Socrates to death. Galileo escaped a similar fate by recanting, and Giordana Bruno, wrestling with his conscience, ultimately chose condemnation rather than deny the truth as he saw it. Even in North America the contemporary attitude of mind that we label McCarthyism (in tribute to its most notable exponent) has caused disquiet among thoughtful men.

Absolute freedom of thought has seldom existed in any country or during any century. There are limits beyond which society is not willing to have the thinkers wander— and there can be no question that the limits in Russia today are much narrower than they are in the West. Karl Marx was allowed to live comfortably in London while he wrote and published the works that are the foundations of modern Communism. Lenin enjoyed similar privileges in England and in Switzerland. No scholar who wrote such bitter critiques of the society in which he lived would enjoy similar opportunities in any part of the U.S.S.R. at the present time. When one thinks of the public criticism of Boris Pasternak for daring to put into the mouth of *Dr. Zhivago* words criticizing the men who won the October Revolution, it is interesting to contemplate the fate of any modern philosopher in the U.S.S.R. who, emulating Karl Marx, wrote three large volumes to analyse the defects of the society in which he lived, to deny that Communism was a satisfactory way of life and to prophesy that it would inevitably disappear from the face of the earth!

Russian thinkers outside of the physical sciences enjoy less freedom of thought and discussion than is to be found in western countries. I suspect that this is partially true even in the physical sciences, although in this field access to foreign information is easy and originality is encouraged. I am confident that it is true in the social sciences and the humanities, where none but the privileged members of institutions of higher education has regular and easy access to books, magazines or newspapers published outside the U.S.S.R.

One cannot, however, stop at this point, as though we were contrasting black and white. One of the significant things about Russia is that there is more freedom of thought today than there was ten years ago. One man, talking to me about English Literature, said, "Five years ago I read your George Orwell's *1984*. It made my hair stand on end. It was so true, but how could he have known it so well when he did not live here?" It is less true today. Boris Pasternak, I understand, is still living quietly at his dacha in spite of the condemnation of his work, and other writers previously condemned are now back in favour.

All things are relative. The man living in Russia realizes with profound relief that thought and discussion are freer today than they were in 1950. Whether conditions will return to the dark night of oppression and regimentation, or continue to develop toward still greater freedom, I do not know. I have no gift of prophecy. It is my own opinion that the present educational effort of Russia, which encourages millions of able young men and women to think, to ask questions, to discuss ideas, will make it harder and harder as the years go by for any future government to impose upon human thought the regimentation that Stalin imposed during the later years of his life. Only the passage of time can show whether that hypothesis is sound.